OBJECT-CENTERED
CHILDREN'S SERMONS

OBJECT-CENTERED CHILDREN'S SERMONS

C. W. BESS

BAKER BOOK HOUSE

Grand Rapids, Michigan 49516

Acknowledgments

Ideas may be conceived mature and full-grown, but books may not be. This volume owes much to the friendship and shared inspiration of Dr. Roy E. DeBrand, pastor of First Baptist Church in Richmond, Texas. Roy and I have "brainstormed" our ideas together for years. While these are my own sermons for children, they represent a style we have developed together.

Encouragement from my family was essential to this ambition. My wife Mary has remained loyal and loving to my own love of writing. Her parents, the C. T. Bushes from Athens, Texas, have provided generous enouragement. My secretary and typist, Mrs. Billy Perry, has been most efficient.

Grateful appreciation is expressed to the Executive Committee of the Southern Baptist Convention for permission to include my previously published sermons from *The Baptist Program*.

Preface

Following World War II our veterans returned home to resume a long neglected home life. The great, postwar baby boom began, but it was accompanied by a curious social phenomenon. With children now everywhere, it seemed that landlords didn't care to rent housing to families with children.

Added to the familiar "For Rent" sign was the message, "No Children Please." We can understand the prohibition of pets, but "No Children"? Surely our local churches would never prohibit children.

But in a way, our traditional worship service geared to adult needs has in many ways discouraged children almost as effectively as a "No Children" sign would. What can we do to remedy this situation? Let us remember our Lord's example.

Our Lord encouraged the little children to come to Him. When the serious-minded disciples felt that the children had claimed too much of His time, Jesus actually rebuked His chosen leaders:

> But when Jesus saw it he was indignant, and said to them, "Let the children come to me, do not hinder them; for to such belongs the kingdom of God (Mark 10:14, RSV).

This remains one of the most tender scenes in the Bible. Jesus leaned over, took children into His arms, laid His hands on them, and blessed them. I believe children still need that personal attention from their pastors and teachers.

This book is sent forth with the prayer that more pastors will invite children to come for a special message during the traditional worship services. Teachers of Sunday school, vacation Bible school, and separate worship services for children will find some help in these pages. When the children come, welcome them!

Contents

Unit 1
Preparing for the Children's Sermon

1.

Opportunity in the Children's Sermon

Nothing is so powerful as an idea whose time has come. As a mode of communication and worship, the children's sermon may not be a recent innovation, but judging from its current popularity, here is an idea whose time has truly come. From large Roman Catholic congregations to small, rural Baptist churches, and every type church between, the children's sermon is becoming a familiar part of the worship service.

Is this a mere fad or does the trend rest on a deeper foundation of need? I believe it reflects a renewed and healthy emphasis on our children. Not only in churches, but everywhere in our culture, children are given more individual attention. The typical child is reared in a smaller family today, attends smaller classes in school, and receives more individual instruction. Parents have always considered children special, but they now have more time and affluence to lavish upon the younger generation.

In contrast, Sunday's congregation is growing larger in size and more formal in worship. Except in churches with aggressive bus ministries, children are becoming the lonely minority in worship services. Too often they feel that the hour is wasted because they are overlooked in content and participation.

The children's sermon therefore meets the special need of the younger mind and active body too long overlooked in our worship pattern geared to adults. Scheduled most often before the offertory hymn, it provides a welcome change. There is activity in walking down the aisle and crowding together on the floor or platform. Informality, participation, and personal attention are provided. This is good. It is the children's special time in the language they love best—simple, short, and spiritual!

For these reasons, the pastor or associate considering the possibility of a children's sermon can be assured of good reception. Even most adults confess to an unusual interest and enjoyment in the children's message. Frequently a parent is overheard saying, "Now that children's sermon was for me! I could understand it all!"

Of course the focus is on the children, since they are your first opportunity for ministry through the children's sermon. Pastor, they are the sweetest, more impressionable, noncritics you will ever have. Because you can lay a foundation for lifetime ministry, the rewards are too great to ignore.

Not only do the children receive firsthand and personalized teaching of God's truths, but they also find in the occasion their first active participation in public worship. They individually respond by coming forward toward the pastor. They realize that a message and a blessing awaits them. The altar area becomes a familiar, yet profound place of life-changing instruction. We pray that later the child will walk down these same aisles for a life-changing commitment with God.

The Interest Object

How do you begin a children's sermon? My method is simple. Every children's sermon is introduced by an interest object which serves to attract attention and focus interest. Even though I choose only familiar and simple items, the children respond with curiosity.

Simple and familiar items common to a child's experiences prove best for this purpose. Remember, you are not teaching children about the object, but are using the object to help illustrate basic truths of God. Therefore avoid any object which would need an elaborate explanation.

Avoid the other extreme of using dramatic objects which would be so interesting that the aroused attention could not be easily channeled into a teaching situation. There is danger in the informal setting of losing control of the situation. Children are thrilled with the freedom to enter the action of a pastor's sermon; and they will do just that. This is good, but you must maintain complete control.

My congregation still remembers the bedlam at our altar when I weighed some jelly beans on an oldtime balance. The principle of God's measured judgment according to His perfect balances (Dan. 5:27) was lost amid a mad scramble for candy accidently spilled.

Not quite so embarrassing, but more frustrating, was the occasion when my interest object, a shoe box full of baby jack rabbits, proved *too* interesting. In a flash little rabbits were in little hands. Too late I realized that nothing is so captivating to children as baby jack rabbits. I doubt if they heard a word of my sermon on God's special protection for all His creatures, and they wouldn't return the rabbits until the sermon was over.

If your interest object is somewhat more interesting than usual, it is wise to arrange help in removing it immediately after the children's sermon. I realized this on the same morning that I finally got back my box of rabbits. Without thought I placed them behind the pulpit as always. Even though the rabbits were completely out of sight, they weren't out of mind. Fortunately they did not escape, but later the benediction was somewhat hurried as I sensed the rush of children for another chance at the rabbits.

One final thought is important when choosing an interest object. Remember to keep the subject just as simple as the object. A common mirror, for example, loses its simplicity if the children's sermon is too abstract.

We adults understand how a transparent glass becomes a mirror when the back is coated with silver. Even a teenager can readily grasp the point that our windows (eyes) to a needy world can be obstructed by money or materialism (silver) so that we see only ourselves in the glass. Beware! The normal child under ten years of age just cannot effectively comprehend this spiritual application. Therefore, choose simple objects and keep the application simple.

Stay with Scripture

Once the interest object has caught the children's attention the pastor should lead naturally into a basic truth. The teaching ought to be simple and short because it summarizes the truth of Scripture. Many pastors find it a helpful discipline to reduce the sermon to an outline form with emphasis on this summary sentence. If you cannot write this main truth in clear and brief words, how can you ever hope to preach it in a child's language?

Next, relate the object to the truth of God's Word. I would emphasize strongly that a children's sermon is like any other sermon. It *must* be based on Scripture. Otherwise the session will be no different than a storytime or object lesson.

Many books on children's sermons today have interesting lessons based on objects with a random Scripture text apparently added as an afterthought. But this should not be so. Preaching must rest on a foundation of God's Word. In my own files are many good ideas which have yet to be "preached" for lack of a strong, simple Scripture text as a basis.

The final element of the sermon is what I choose to call a "memory maker." It may be an object which is directly related to the children's sermon such as an apple, pencil, or some other simple thing. Very often it takes the form of a tract or printed text. Sometimes I even summarize the outline of the sermon with printed text.

The purpose of the memory maker is to encourage the children to explain the sermon at home. Often I receive helpful hints from parents reporting how children confused the truth presented. The feedback is valuable to my own skills, especially when I plan to repeat the sermon later. Often I find that the sermon just didn't reach the children as I had hoped.

When the child does understand the truth, his memory maker helps in further impressing it in his mind and heart. Then as he retells the story, he is assisted by a memory aid. Sometimes this is the only way God's precious promises can ever be presented to the parents who never come to church.

In summary, the structure of the children's sermon ought to be built around the Scripture text. The standard format I have developed includes: (1) *an interest object* leading to (2) *a main truth* supported by (3) *a simple text*. When possible I send the children back to their pews with (4) *a memory maker*.

4o

Should Preschoolers Be Included?

The children's sermon is obviously more difficult to present, and the children more difficult to control whenever preschoolers are included. Should the occasion therefore be limited to school-age children only?

Some pastors establish a minimum age of six years. They consider the children's sermon to be genuine and serious preaching which requires both attention and perception. Children who are accustomed to a structured, learning situation can better respond to the opportunity.

Besides creating a better learning situation for the child's perspective, the older group simplifies the pastor's preparation. Ask any seasoned writer or teacher of preschool materials! The younger the age, the more difficult the task to reduce an adult world to preschool level.

Remember that whatever age span your group includes, the sermon should be understandable by the youngest children of that group. The inclusion of the preschool children then rules out many potential sermons based on interest objects and truths too abstract for them. It thus complicates a pastor's preparation.

For these reasons the pastor planning children's sermons as a regular feature might best begin with older children first. The well of creative but simple ideas runs dry too soon even without the limitation of the younger group.

The pastor who chooses this safer approach of school-age children only should carefully explain his reasons in a positive way. Make promotion day a wonderful occasion by honoring the first time participants. Let preschoolers look forward to that day. This may help them understand the requirement.

On the other hand, including the preschooler opens the door wider to greater opportunities. Parents of four-year-olds in my church seem genuinely grateful. The four-year-old needs the activity of walking down the aisle. The harried parents themselves need those few minutes when I personally take charge of their children who are learning that "big church" can last for a very long hour.

Visitors and prospects seem impressed with a children's sermon which includes their preschooler. Often this makes the difference to a family being willing to attend our worship service the first time.

Therefore, though it means more preparation on my part, I have chosen to include the preschool child. I personally treasure these moments as an opportunity to cement affectionate ties between pastor and children. I want even these preschoolers to understand that I am always available to them as their pastor. Who knows? If I can relate to them on the preschool level, perhaps they will remember and lend me an ear during their teenage years!

How often should the children's sermon be offered? Schedules vary from monthly to weekly. I have found that every other week fits better into my own pattern. The children and their parents would gladly make it weekly, but fifty-two sermons a year on the more difficult preschool level is more than I can creatively produce.

Where Shall I Stand?

By its very nature, the children's sermon presents the pastor with one choice he doesn't have when he stands behind the pulpit. Just where will he stand? He will definitely not stand behind the pulpit and preferably not even on the elevated platform. If this is to be "their" sermon, surely the children deserve to meet their pastor at their own level. Even children are sensitive to this symbolic gesture.

Allow the children to help decide where they are most comfortable. Some will choose the first pew and others the floor or the steps. The alert pastor then chooses his place most convenient in their midst.

Should the speaker stand or sit among the children? In a small group teaching situation it is almost always recommended that a speaker get down on the physical level of preschoolers, but don't forget that many adults are enjoying the children's sermon too. Unless the speaker is exceptionally tall his standing will not penalize his presentation. However, a high stool might be effective in some cases as a compromise.

Avoid notes, a lectern, and a floor microphone since the pastor should be free to move from child to child. Keep the hands free to display and hold the interest objects. Be yourself. This will keep the children's interest focused upon the pastor and his message.

In many churches a public address system is not needed during the worship hour. For the children's sermon, however, a lapel microphone will help project the softer conversational tones normally used in talking to children. Remember that the adults seated in the rear pews deserve to hear clearly, too.

Where Can I Find New Ideas?

Every experienced preacher knows that the most difficult part of sermon preparation is choosing ideas and texts. But once past the struggle of choosing the right sermon ideas, we can easily develop them into sermons.

Remember that simplicity is the watchword for all children's sermons. The idea should not be complex. If it must be explained in detail, it then loses its force.

In addition to the simple idea, the child also seeks familiarity. Common articles of life such as a shoe, apple, candle, flashlight, etc. are better than the engineer's slide rule. Often my young son will bring some possession like a balloon or a key and suggest, "Dad, this would make a good children's sermon." Of course, he doesn't provide a text or a basic truth, but most ideas can be developed with some creative brooding. I have discovered these home-inspired sermons to be far more effective than the suggestions of most books which usually aim at the older child.

The world of children seems to provide the best key in searching for valid and helpful ideas. For the pastor whose children are already grown it becomes imperative that he somehow maintain contact with these little ones. Perhaps some frequent visits to the preschool children's department in Sunday school might help. Play with these children and observe their interests.

You might investigate your local bookstore for ideas. An early pioneer of children's sermons was G. B. F. Hallock. Although most of these are out of print, any seminary library or long-established church library might have these.

Many new books on children's sermons are being published each year. While most of these books offer a multitude of ideas, it is regrettable that the majority neglect a scriptural foundation. Most are more correctly classified as object lesson books. Read these anyway to spark your own ideas and adaptations. Since most are aimed at the nine- to twelve-year-old level, you must remember to either adapt or disregard those ideas that are too advanced for your younger children. To find out your children's specific levels of understanding, consult age-graded literature developed by professionals in your own demomination.

Don't neglect one of the most fertile fields for new ideas. Swap ideas with a pastor friend who enjoys preaching children's sermons in his church. What works in developing adult sermon ideas can help with children's sermons, too.

Unit 2
Children's Sermons

1.

From Bad to Good

Interest Object:	A cluster of grapes and a small box of raisins
Main Truth:	God can change something bad into something good.
Scripture Text:	"We know that in everything God works for good with those who love him, who are called according to his purpose" (Rom. 8:28, RSV).
Memory Maker:	Small boxes of raisins

"You children can see that in my hand I have a cluster of grapes. Nearly everybody likes sweet grapes, but until these modern days of refrigeration we had no way to keep grapes fresh. Most grapes grown in the old days were therefore made into wine.

"Back in 1872 a terrible drought kept California grapes from growing big like these. The grape growers were saddened at the sight of their vineyards having such poor grapes. Rather than trying to make wine, one grower sent a box full of the shriveled grapes to a grocer in San Francisco. He instructed the man to sell them at any price. Now what could a grocer do with a box of bad grapes?

"That's a question God must sometime consider. He sees boys and girls who do bad things. Can anything good come from children like that?

"Do you know what that grocer did with those dried grapes? He left them in the sun a couple days longer, and he discovered raisins! [Pastor drops the cluster of grapes into a box or bag and pulls out a box of raisins.] Dried grapes turn into raisins. In this way the grape-raising industry of California was born. What had seemed like a terrible disaster had turned into a wonderful discovery. Now grapes could be grown not only for wine, but for raisins also.

"That's the way God works too. In Romans 8:28 we have this great promise: 'We know that in everything God works for good with those who love him, who are called according to his purpose.' Good can come out of bad. But notice who can claim this promise. It is to those who love the Lord and are called according to His purpose. We must love God and belong to Him before we ask Him to make good from bad."

Giving and Receiving

Interest Object:	An unprimed pump set in an antique cream can
Main truth:	If we are to receive, we must also give.
Scripture Text:	"Give, and it will be given to you; good measure, pressed down, shaken together, running over . . ." (Luke 6:38, RSV).
Memory Maker:	A paper cutout of a pump with the text printed on it

Notes and Preparation

Children are fascinated by pumps, so your extra effort in preparing this interest object will be well rewarded. In my case, I explained the idea to several members whom I suspected would have a pump or an old cream can. One deacon agreed that his wife had always wanted an old pump and cream can combination. He prepared this for our children and later gave it to his wife.

Fill the bottom of the cream can with sufficient water not only to pump, but also for extra weight, so the pump won't be top-heavy in the can. Also have ready one cup of water plus a small empty bucket.

As the children assemble, let them examine the pump set in the can. Explain how a pump works and allow volunteers to pump some water in a small can. Trying as hard as they can pump, the children are not successful in pumping water from an unprimed pump. At this point the pastor explains the scriptural truth that they can't always be receivers without sometimes being givers. Jesus promised us in Luke 6:38 that if we give so that God and others receive, then we shall also receive. Giving often comes before receiving.

Illustrate this by pouring into the pump one cup of water. (In your prior preparation be sure that the pump suck is still wet and that the single cup of water does indeed prime this pump.) Now the pump is primed. The children will be excited and will themselves observe that the pump returns far more than it originally received. The cup of water now fills a bucket!

Tell the children that we must be both givers and receivers. To receive we must also give. This is not a selfish truth to be used to get more, but to make us realize we must give more.

𝕯₀

A Body Like a Church

Interest Object: A model of a church house or a large picture of a typical church building

Main Truth: Treat your body with the respect due God's house because your body is a temple for God.

Scripture Text: "Do you not know that your body is a temple of the Holy Spirit within you, which you have from God? You are not your own; you were bought with a price. So glorify God in your body" (I Cor. 6:19-20, RSV).

"What does a church house look like? Most of us think of a building like this model I hold before you. It has a white steeple and stained glass windows. But many churches do not look like this. Some churches are made of beautiful brick, while others are simple buildings, without walls, only a roof. Some are large and others small. Each church is different, yet has the same purpose for being.

"A building becomes a church not through stained glass windows nor a steeple, but only when people use that place to worship God. It becomes God's house. That is why we are so respectful and reverent when we enter a church. We try to take special care of this building because it is God's house.

29

"Let me tell you about another place where God lives that needs very special care. This special church house of which I am thinking belongs only to you and to God. God lives in your church. Listen to this Scripture from I Corinthians 6: 'Do you not know that your body is a temple of the Holy Spirit within you, which you have from God?'

"The Bible says that your body is a temple or a church where God lives within you. This means that your body is not your own; it belongs to God. Therefore we must take good care of this body.

"This is the very reason why we believe it is wrong to smoke tobacco products or to eat so much that our body becomes very fat. That would not be taking care of God's church where He lives. We are to live our lives so that our bodies will be healthy and that God will be glorified through our bodies."

4.

An Empty Life

Interest Object:	Extra large firecracker
Main Truth:	We are empty, powerless, and worthless until we have Jesus inside us.
Scripture Truth:	"Behold, I stand at the door and knock; if anyone hears my voice and opens the door, I will come in to him . . ." (Rev. 3:20, RSV).

Notes and Preparation

Children are fascinated by firecrackers. Secure a small cardboard tube about the size of a toilet tissue center. Plug the top with a bottle cork and insert a string or fuse into it. Paint the firecracker a bright red, but leave the bottom very obviously open. At the right time you will then reveal an empty shell representing the empty life without Jesus.

"See my giant firecraker? This morning let's light it so we can hear the biggest bang ever! I'll set it up here out of the way. After I light it you must hold your hands over your ears. It will make a big noise. [Pastor lights the fuse and everyone waits. Nothing happens.]

"What happened? This big firecracker didn't even explode. I wonder why? [The pastor absent-mindedly turns the firecracker over so the children can see through the bottom that it is only an empty shell. The children will delightfully inform the pastor of this fact!]

"This firecracker is nothing but an empty shell. There is nothing inside of it to make it worthwhile. Did you know that some people are just like this empty shell? The Bible teaches us that our lives are empty until Jesus enters. He will not come into any life until He is asked to enter. Jesus wants us to invite Him into our hearts. Then He will live inside of us forever.

"One of my favorite texts is found in Revelation 3:20. This verse tells me that Jesus knocks on the outside of my heart door wanting in. [Read text and summarize the truth.]"

5.

A New Heart

Interest Object:	A man's wrist watch
Main Truth:	God wants to give you a new heart so you can live forever.
Scripture Text:	"A new heart also will I give you . . ." (Ezek. 36:26a).

Notes and Preparation

A telephone and a ringing sound of the telephone are required for this sermon. Any telephone attached to a telephone jack can be removed. For the ringing sound you might consider installing a battery operated bell. Otherwise a cassette recorder with the taped sounds of a ringing telephone will do. The recorder can be hidden in the choir loft for a cooperative choir member to operate.

The use of strange sounding names like Frieblehousenwitz sometimes adds fun for children and adults alike. Develop your own fantasy names if this proves popular.

As the pastor is welcoming the children, the ringing sound of a telephone is heard. The pastor quickly explains how he had a new telephone installed in his pulpit. Then he goes to answer it. The conversation begins:

"Oh, hello, Mr. Frieblehousenwitz. No, you didn't disturb me. I was just preparing to tell my children about our sermon for today. [Holding his hand over the mouthpiece the pastor explains quickly to the children. The day before he had left a message for this watch repair expert.]

"Yes, about my watch—it just won't run anymore. It starts and stops, but most of the time it just plays dead. [Pause] What brand is it? Let me look. It's a Snitzenbloober special. I bought it about a year ago for five dollars. [Pause] Oh, you already know what's wrong with it? How can you? [Pause] So you have a book that explains what's wrong with this brand of watch. And the book says that after one year the battery must be replaced.

"Now I remember. My watch runs on a tiny battery so I never have to wind it. [Pause, then to children] He says my watch needs a new type of battery that will last and last and last. [Resumes conversation] Well, I don't know, Mr. Frieblehousenwitz. I don't have much money [Pause] You really mean it? You will install a new battery free? Thank you! I'll see you this afternoon! Goodbye."

[The pastor hangs up the telephone and discusses further with the children how nice the man is for giving him a new battery free. Then he presents the obvious comparison and application to our own lives.] "Each of us is born with a heart of flesh not designed to run forever. We have a book that explains all about it—the Bible. The Bible teaches us that each one of us must someday be born again. It's like getting a brand new heart so we can live forever.

"Long ago God told Ezekiel to promise this new heart to his people. 'A new heart also will I give you. . . .' Today Jesus can come into our hearts too and make us new."

Erasing Sin

Interest Object:	Pencil with eraser on the end
Main Truth:	We are not perfect, but God can erase our sins.
Scripture Text:	"Have mercy on me, O God, . . . blot out my transgressions" (Ps. 51:1, RSV). "Hide thy face from my sins, and blot out all mine iniquities" (Ps. 51:9, RSV). "Repent ye therefore, and be converted, that your sins may be blotted out, . . ." (Acts 3:19).
Memory Maker:	A pencil with eraser for each child

Notes and Preparation

A common pencil with an eraser on the end serves this simple, yet forceful truth. The pastor asks the children the purpose of the rubber tip attached to his pencil. Be sure to give them time to think and realize that erasers are for mistakes. Nail down the truth that no one is perfect. Therefore we all need erasers.

You can further illustrate this truth by the strange fact that even ballpoint pens which write in permanent ink sell better with an eraser attached. Experts say the eraser is comforting to have even if it is not usable with permanent ink.

"The eraser reminds us that we make mistakes. The Bible says that all of us sin. It's so hard to say, 'I'm sorry.' When we do something wrong, God wants us to ask His forgiveness. Then a wonderful thing happens. When we ask for God's forgiveness, He wipes away our sin.

"Once the great King David committed a terrible sin. He felt so bad about it that he asked God to forgive him and erase that sin from his life. He felt very sorry about it. Listen to a few words of his prayer in Psalm 51: 'Have mercy on me, O God . . . blot out my transgressions' (v. 1, RSV). 'Hide thy face from my sins, and blot out all mine iniquities.' (v. 9, RSV).

"David wanted his sins erased. We're glad that God does forgive us whenever we become so sorry that we sincerely ask Him to."

7.

God Can Count Better

Interest Object: A variety of small adding machines and calculators.

Main Truth: God counts better and remembers longer than any machine, because he knows us and never forgets us.

Scripture Text: "In the meantime, when so many thousands of the multitude had gathered together that they trod upon one another, he began to say to his disciples first. . . . Are not five sparrows sold for two pennies? And not one of them is forgotten before God. Why, even the hairs of your head are all numbered" (Luke 12:2, 6-7a, RSV).

"You are certainly a fine and large group of children crowded around me. You are almost too many for me to count. When I was small, I used to count on my fingers, but now I can use these new adding machines. Some of these are called calculators because they add and multiply large numbers. Some even have a special memory button which helps us to add different groups of numbers at the same time. These machines count and remember.

"Did you know that God counts better and remembers longer than any machine? God also knows your names, where you live, and everything about you. He even knows how many hairs are on your head! God knows everything and never forgets anything.

"It makes no difference how many children and adults come to God. He knows us, counts us, and never forgets. In Luke 12 we have the description of a great crowd. So many people had come to hear Jesus that they stepped on each other's toes. Jesus used the occasion to teach them this important lesson.

"He told them that God never forgets anyone. [Read Scripture here.] He counts better than any machine."

8.

A Favor for a Friend

Interest Object:	Motel doorknob sign
Main Truth:	Jesus is our friend who wants to do good favors for us when we do what He asks.
Scripture Text:	"You are my friends if you do what I command you. . . . But I chose you and appointed you that you should go and bear fruit . . . so that whatever you ask the Father in my name, he may give it to you" (John 15:14, 16, RSV).

"Do you recognize this sign which comes from a motel? On one side it says, 'Please do not disturb.' If you want to take a nap in the afternoon or want to sleep late the next morning, you simply hang this little sign on the other side of the door. People who see this sign will realize that you do not want to be disturbed, so they will not knock.

"The other side of the sign says, 'Maid service please.' This means just the opposite. Instead of wanting to be left alone, you want a favor. Perhaps you have run out of soap or clean towels. So by placing this sign on the same doorknob you are asking a favor.

"Some people treat God this same way. Whenever God wants them to do something good like visiting the sick, teaching a Sunday school class, or giving to His church, they reply to God, 'Please do not disturb.' Yet if they want something from God, they very quickly say to God, 'Maid service please.'

"Jesus taught us, 'You are my friends if you do what I command you.' Now what does Jesus command of us? In the same lesson in John 15, 16 we have the answer. '. . . But I chose you and appointed you that you should go and bear fruit. . . .' This is just another way of saying that we are supposed to do as we are told. If we obey His commands then we are allowed to ask anything. '. . . So that whatever you ask the Father in my Name, he may give it to you.' "

𝒟₉.

The Light of the World

Interest Object: A heavy-duty flashlight plus a light bulb within a socket attached by cord to an electrical outlet

Main Truth: You are the light of the world, but only God can give you power for that light.

Scripture Text: "Let your light so shine before men, that they may see. . . . But you shall receive power . . ." (Matt. 5:16; Acts 1:8, RSV).

"Jesus told us that each one of us ought to be a light to shine before others that they might see. Here is a heavy-duty flashlight which gives a very fine light to help others see. At night I could help someone to his car. I might be able to help you sometime to see a coin that you dropped in the dark. This flashlight is very handy to have.

"Here is another kind of light very familiar to all of us. It is a light bulb which gives a very steady light also. But this light is attached to a cord which is plugged into an electrical outlet. As long as the light bulb is plugged into the power source, it will continue to give light. But it cannot burn by itself. It must be plugged in.

"Can you imagine the flashlight making fun of this light bulb by saying, 'I'm sorry that you can't go where I go. My power is within myself. You have to stay connected to a power source.'

"Ah, but the light bulb has the last laugh. Do you know why? Of course. The flashlight which burns on its own power will very soon burn itself out. The light bulb will continue to burn on and on.

"Our lives are just like these lights. Jesus commanded us to shine. [Read Matthew 5:16.] We cannot shine very long with our own light. We must be plugged in to God so that our light will shine and shine. The source of our power to shine comes from God. [Read Acts 1:8.]"

10.

The Praying Hands
of a Friend

Interest Object: A plaster mold or picture of the *Praying Hands*

Main Truth: True friends are faithful to love one another always.

Scripture Text: "A friend loves at all times" (Prov. 17:17a, RSV).

"Here is a reproduction of a famous work. What do you think these hands are doing? They are held in the position of prayer. Let me tell you the story behind this famous scene.

"About the time that Columbus discovered America, two young men in Germany discovered the meaning of friendship. They were searching not for new lands but for fame and fortune as artists. Yet they were too poor to attend the great art schools of the world.

"They made an agreement that one would work hard and pay for the other's schooling. Franz Knigstein agreed to work hard so that his friend Albrecht Dürer could study. They planned for Albrecht to study art and become successful with enough money that Franz could then study. Years passed and Albrecht learned so well that he became very famous as a great artist. He finally had enough money to repay his good friend. He hurried back home to tell Franz that he could quit working and start studying to become a famous artist himself.

"But it was too late now for Franz to become a great artist. During the years of hard work his hands and fingers became stiff and twisted. No longer could he paint the fine, delicate brush strokes of beautiful painting. It was too late.

"Some men would have become very angry and bitter, but not Franz. He was a true friend to Albrecht. One day Albrecht dropped by his friend's home and saw him kneeling in prayer. His gnarled hands were folded praying for his friend who was now a famous artist. Albrecht never forgot the sacrifice of his friend nor the moment of that prayer. He created this beautiful work of art to remember the friend who had loved him at all times.

"Friends are very important. The Bible tells us that a friend loves us at all times. Will you try being that kind of friend to others?"

11.

Good or Bad?

Interest Object: A long-stemmed match which is ignited

Main Truth: Like a fire the tongue can be either good or bad.

Scripture Text: "So the tongue is a little member and boasts of great things. How great a forest is set ablaze by a small fire! And the tongue is a fire" (James 3:5-6a, RSV). "And every tongue [shall] confess that Jesus Christ is Lord, to the glory of God the Father" (Phil. 2:11, RSV).

"Don't play with matches! How often have you heard your parents say this? Here is a match which I will strike. Now is this fire on the match good or bad?

"That all depends. Everything in nature has two different uses. It can be used for good or it can be used for bad. For example, the reason it is dangerous to play with matches is that you could start a fire which could burn your home. It might even burn you. That is bad. On the other hand, aren't you glad that fire helps cook our food? Fire is very useful in making metal for our cars and plastics for our drinking cups. Fire is often very useful.

"That's the way it is with your tongue. The Bible tells us that the little tongue can sometimes be like a very bad fire which rages through the forest burning everything. That is bad. Any time you speak harsh words at someone or tell a lie, it's the same as your tongue starting a fire. That's bad.

"We must be very careful of what we say. We don't want to start bad fires with our tongues. How much better it is to say good things with our tongue. The Bible teaches us that the best things our tongues can ever say is that Jesus is Lord."

12.

No Secret Sin

Interest Object: A felt stamp pad with hand stamp

Main Truth: Sin in our lives will always be discovered, because with God there is no secret sin.

Scripture Text: "And be sure your sin will find you out" (Num. 32:23b, RSV).

"Have you ever gone to a large amusement park or a ball game where you paid an admission price? Perhaps later you discovered your lunch was left in the car. Naturally you didn't want to pay again, so as you left, a man used a stamp on your hand like this. Then when you returned, you had proof that you had already paid, so he let you in. The ink mark on your hand was proof that you were there earlier.

"A young man was once employed after school as a part-time helper in a post office. A few days later some money was missing from the cash drawer. One day after some more money was missed, a postal inspector appeared to investigate.

"He asked all the employees to do something unusual. Everyone lined up side by side wondering what would happen. Each employee was asked to show his empty hands before a special purple light.

"The inspector explained that the day before some of their money had been treated with invisible chemicals. Whoever touched the money or took it would have a stain on his hands which could not be washed off.

"Everyone gasped when the young man extended his hands. They glowed with an unmistakable color under the light. All he could say was, 'I tried to wash it off, but I couldn't.'

"God has said, 'Be sure your sins will find you out.' Whenever you sin, your life will bear the marks of sin. In the light of God's judgment, no sin is ever secret."

13.

Ears to Hear

Interest Object: A collection of dolls

Main Truth: Only humans, because they are created by God, can listen and obey.

Scripture Text: "He who has ears, let him hear" (Matt. 13:9, RSV).

Notes and Preparation

Dolls have always been important to children, but never before have they been so life-like. A week or two ahead ask the first or second grade girls to bring a favorite doll to church. Ask especially for the dolls that walk, talk, wet, eat, or do some other life-like thing. The boys can bring their G. I. Joe dolls.

"I have asked some of you to bring your favorite dolls this morning. These dolls are fascinating because they act almost like people. Some walk and some talk, some eat and some wet. G. I. Joe even fights. [The pastor can take a moment to admire these individual dolls or interview some of the children.]

"I surely hope that the makers of dolls will never create a doll that does everything you boys and girls can do. If that happens, we probably won't have any more children in the world! Mothers and dads would surely prefer a doll that talks and walks and never does anything bad. They wouldn't want children anymore!

"Do you think that would ever happen? I don't. You know why? Because people can never create anything quite like you children. You are different because you can do things that dolls will never do. A doll may have ears but it cannot hear. If it cannot hear, it cannot obey its maker.

"God could have decided to make only robot dolls instead of real boys and girls. The robot dolls would never have done any wrong like people do. Yet people can listen to God. Because we have ears to hear, we can therefore obey God and love Him.

"That's exactly what Jesus told us so often. Jesus said, 'He who has ears, let him hear.' Some people act like they never hear God. They never do what He wants them to do. Wouldn't it be nice if everyone would hear God and obey Him?"

14.

Free Because God Pays

Interest Object:	A newspaper grocery advertisement
Main Truth:	All good blessings of God are free to us only because God has already paid the price.
Scripture Text:	"Say there! Is anyone thirsty? Come and drink—even if you have no money! Come, take your choice of wine and milk—it's all free!" (Isa. 55:1, LB).
Memory Maker:	A sack of candy

Notes and Preparation

A grocery ad from the daily newspaper can be prepared by printing in large red letters "FREE CANDY*." The asterisk is duplicated at the bottom of the page with the explanation, "Free with $10.00 purchase." Sacks of individually wrapped candies can be given to the children as a memory maker.

"Holding the newspaper advertisement for everyone to see, the pastor asks the children to read the good news. There is free candy at this grocery store near by. Most of us can get very excited over a free offer such as candy. Let's say you rush on down to the grocery store and ask for your free candy. Do you know what will happen?

"The clerk will say, 'But didn't you read the fine print?' And then we look at the bottom of the page. It says that the candy is free only if we purchase ten dollars' worth of groceries. But we don't have any money. Does that mean that we can't have the free candy?

"Let us further pretend that as we are standing there, we see a neighbor who ought to be very mad at you. Perhaps you were playing ball with some children the day before and broke his window. When he sees you, he might be very angry.

"But this neighbor does a wonderful thing. Instead of being mad at you, he calls you over and places his hand on your shoulder. He says, 'I have just purchased more than ten dollars' worth of groceries. Because I love you, I'm going to ask the manager if he will give you the free candy.' Wouldn't that be wonderful?

"Did you know that is the very same way God deals with us? We do not deserve to have any of His free gifts, but He has already paid the price for us. He offers us free salvation if we only trust Him.

"In the Old Testament a prophet named Isaiah spoke for God concerning the free gift. It's free because God has paid the price! Let's read about it in Isaiah 55:1."

15.

The Perfect Cleaning

Interest Object:	A beautiful china plate and three separate cleaning cloths.
Main Truth:	Because Jesus was perfect, without sin, He is able to cleanse us.
Scripture Text:	"[He] was in all points tempted like as we are, yet without sin" (Heb. 4:15b).

"Do you ever help your mother set the table? Perhaps your mother likes to use her best china whenever company comes. Let's pretend that you are helping her set the table and discover a spot on a plate. Now what must you do?

"To clean a plate we need some type of cleaning cloth. [Pastor holds up the first cloth which has dark, dirty stains on it. Black ink can be used earlier to prepare this effect.] Would you use this kind of cloth? Definitely not.

"What about this second cloth? It looks clean so let's use it. [This cloth should be secretly prepared with a small amount of shoe polish in wax form carefully concealed inside. With a little practice you can take a cloth which looks clean and make the plate look very dirty.] Wait a minute. Something is wrong with this cloth. Even though it first looked clean, it was very dirty.

"What kind of cloth can clean a plate? Of course! A cloth must be clean itself before it can clean something else. Let's look carefully at this third cloth. It looks clean, [Pastor polishes the plate] and indeed it is. It cleans the plate quite well.

"Did you know that all of us do wrong things, and thus become very soiled and dirty within our lives. This is called sin. No one can clean us from sin, because no other person is perfect and sinless. Only God can forgive sin, because through Jesus Christ, He came into our world and was perfect. In Hebrews 4:15 we are told that Jesus was tempted just like we are, yet was without sin. That means Jesus is a perfect Savior who can forgive us and clean us of our sin."

16.

Dynamite Power

Interest Object: A mock stick of dynamite
Main Truth: Greater even than dynamite is the power of His resurrection.
Scripture Text: "That I may know him and the power of his resurrection . . ." (Phil. 3:10, RSV).

"Can any of you guess what this object represents? It is red and has a string attached which we call a fuse. This represents dynamite. If it were real and we lit the fuse, this entire building would be destroyed.

"Years ago a Swedish inventor named Alfred Nobel discovered the way to make dynamite. He did not really have a name to call his new discovery, but he knew it was very powerful. Just a little dynamite could blow up rocks or tree stumps much easier than digging them out. Here was a very powerful discovery. But what would he call it?

"He decided to make a new word to describe this powerful explosive. He took the Greek word *dunamis,* which meant power. This word power is found often in our Bible. God has power. One of the greatest examples of God's power was demonstrated for us when Jesus was dead. He had the power to conquer death and come back to life. That is called resurrection. Paul the apostle once spoke about this great power. Paul wanted to know all about God and especially about the wonderful power of Christ's resurrection."

17.

Learning to Lose

Interest Object: An empty fish stringer

Main Truth: When we cannot win, let us be good losers.

Scripture Truth: "Master, we toiled all night and took nothing!" (Luke 5:5a, RSV).

"Let me tell you a true 'fish story' from my last fishing trip when I fished late into the night. Here are the results of my effort! [Pastor reaches into pocket and pulls out an empty stringer.]

"You thought I was going to tell you about all the big fish I caught. To tell the truth, I didn't catch any. I failed. I spent all of that time and brought nothing home to show.

"Some people get very frustrated and angry when they don't catch the biggest fish or win first place. Sometimes they kick the dog or say bad words. They do this because they have never learned to lose.

"A good loser is always better than a bad winner. After all, nobody can win all the time. Sometimes in life we have to lose. When that happens, we must be a good loser and wait until next time. There's always tomorrow to win if we have learned to lose gracefully today.

"Jesus once told a fisherman named Simon Peter to take his fishing boat back into the water and let down the nets. Jesus promised his friend Peter a good catch. Peter had been discouraged because he had been a failure the night before. 'Master, we toiled all night and took nothing! But at your word I will let down the nets.'

"Of course, Peter was discouraged. But he had been a good loser. He knew that no one can win all the time, so he was prepared to try again. This time he caught so many fish that he and his friends needed help carrying them back to shore. Learning to lose today can help us in winning tomorrow."

18.

God Remembers

Interest Object:	A cassette tape recorder
Main Truth:	God hears and remembers every secret word we ever say.
Scripture Text:	"Nothing is covered up that will not be revealed, or hidden that will not be known. Whatever you have said in the dark shall be heard in the light, and what you have whispered in private rooms shall be proclaimed upon the housetops" (Luke 12:2-3, RSV).

"Our interest object today is very familiar to children now, although it was very new ten years ago. This is a small tape recorder which is listening to every word we say. Would some of you like to whisper a few words into the microphone?

"Now that we have said a few words for the recorder, can you children remember everything that was said? Can you repeat word for word what we all said? My memory is not that good. But this recorder can remember everything. Let's play it back and listen for just a moment.

"Did you know that God hears everything just like this recorder? God always remembers the words we say in secret. The Bible teaches us that some day every word that we have said will be revealed.

"Nothing is too hard for God. If we are able to make a machine which can remember words, surely God who made us can remember all the bad things we ever say. This teaches us that we must be very careful of what we say. A machine which never forgets, reminds us of a God who always remembers."

19.

Getting the Job Done

Interest Object:	One gleaming, stainless steel knife and one common, carbon steel knife
Main Truth:	Looking good is fine, but doing good is better.
Scripture Text:	"What do you think? A man had two sons; and he went to the first and said, 'Son, go and work in the vineyard today.' And he answered, 'I will not'; but afterward he repented and went. And he went to the second and said the same; and he answered, 'I go, sir,' but he did not go. Which of the two did the will of his father?" (Matt. 21:28-31a, RSV).

"Here in each hand is a knife brought from my kitchen at home. Notice that one knife is made of beautiful gleaming, stainless steel. The other knife is not very pretty. It has some stains and tarnishes on it. Yet do we buy a knife to look at or to use?

"Most of the kitchen knives we buy today are beautiful, gleaming knives of stainless steel—but they are better to look at than to use. If you are looking for a knife to do the job right, then don't look for stainless steel. It looks beautiful, but it doesn't cut as well as this carbon steel blade. Neither does it sharpen well. The carbon knives sometimes get dull and tarnish easy, but in the long run they seldom wear out and are easily sharpened.

"Jesus once told a story about a father with two sons. He commanded them both to go out and work in the vineyard. Now the first son disobeyed his father by saying, 'I will not.' That didn't look very good on his part. Later he felt sorry and went to the field and worked.

"The second son said, 'Yes, I will go.' He looked very good in saying that, but he never did go out and work. His true actions did not match his good appearance.

"The question that Jesus asked was similar to this choice between two knives. Which is better: the one who looks bad, but gets the job done, or the one who looks good, but didn't do the right thing?"

20.

How Do I Look?

Interest Object: Small hand mirror
Main Truth: People on earth look at our outward appearance, but God looks inside at our hearts.
Scripture Text: "Man looks on the outward appearance, but the Lord looks on the heart" (I Sam. 16:7c, RSV).
Memory Maker: A small mirror for each child.

"A mirror helps us keep clean. How else would I know when my face is dirty, when my hair is combed properly, or when my tie is on straight? Most of the time a mirror is very helpful to me.

"Sometimes a mirror makes me very sad when I see my face. I prefer to be handsome or at least that my nose could be smaller and my face prettier. Some people who are very beautiful spend too much time looking in the mirror to admire their good looks.

"In the Bible, God teaches us often that the face is not as important as the heart. Unlike a mirror which shows only the outside, God looks inside the heart.

"Long ago God decided to choose a new king to replace King Saul. God told His prophet Samuel where to look and what kind of man to select. Samuel saw a young man named Eliab who was very handsome. Evidently Eliab was tall and looked very much like a king, because Samuel thought that surely here was the man. Yet God said, 'Do not look on his appearance or on the height of his stature . . . for the Lord sees not as man sees; man looks on the outward appearance, but the Lord looks on the heart.'

"Because this is true, we should never make fun of someone's face. Remember that God sees the heart rather than the face. Also, we should be careful in the thoughts of our hearts because God sees everything within us that others can't see."

21.

Getting What You Want?

Interest Object: A small crab apple
Main Truth: We don't always need what we want.
Scripture Text: ". . . for your Father knoweth what things ye have need of, before ye ask him" (Matt. 6:8).

Notes and Preparation

Almost every pastor can reach back to his childhood memories and retrieve a story like this. Like that famous fruit in the garden of Eden, the crab apple in this story represents our selfish desires. It's what we want and think we need.

Few people today would recognize the small crab apple. Any small, hard, light green apple will serve well. In his own words, the pastor's story may be similar to the following.

"When I was a boy, I enjoyed climbing all trees, but especially apple trees. An apple always tasted better when eaten in a tree. Of course, one must wait until the apples are ripe and ready to be eaten.

"Once when I visited my grandparents, I saw a beautiful apple tree filled with little green apples. My grandfather warned me not to climb in that tree and not to eat those apples. You know what happened? The longer I looked up at those delicious apples, the hungrier I became. Nothing seemed as important as climbing that tree and eating green apples. When nobody was looking, I climbed the tree and ate several apples. They didn't taste as good as I thought and soon I had a terrible tummy ache. I really hadn't been very smart. I knew what I wanted, and I thought that was what I needed. But when I got what I thought I wanted, I decided for sure I didn't want what I got!

"Has something like this ever happened to you? You wanted something so much, but after you got it, you didn't want it. That's why God doesn't give us everything we think we want. Maybe it wouldn't be good for us. Then we wouldn't want it later.

"Let me give another example. Do you like candy? I like it too, but if we had all the candy we ever wanted, our teeth would decay. That means a toothache and a trip to the dentist. We don't like that!

"Jesus once told us that our Father in heaven knows what we need before we ever ask Him. I'm glad. Then when we ask for something which we don't get, we don't have to worry that God didn't hear us. He knows what we want, but He also protects us by sometimes saying no to our desires.

"Jesus promised us that our Father in heaven knows what we *need* even before we ask Him. We can trust God to provide everything He knows we need instead of everything we want."

22.

I Can Do All Things

Interest Object:	A large rubber band
Main Truth:	Alone we are powerless and worthless, but with Jesus we are powerful and worth much.
Scripture Text:	"I can do all things through Christ which strengtheneth me" (Phil. 4:13).

"We have before us this morning a very important little tool called a rubber band. Can you help me decide what can be done with the rubber band? Yes, you boys know that a rubber band can shoot paper wads. We remember that when David was a young lad, he put a band on a stick and killed a giant named Goliath. He used what we call a slingshot.

"Some of you boys use rubber bands to hold the newspapers you deliver each afternoon. Many wind-up toys have a rubber band to help them move. In every office of America, you can find rubber bands working hard to hold packages together. Some factories even use giant rubber bands in packing furniture.

"If we listen carefully, we can almost hear the rubber band saying, 'I can do all things.' But he can't. Look at him. The rubber band is really a lazy sort of fellow who likes nothing better than to curl up in a little circle. By itself it can't do anything.

"The rubber band needs a person to pull and tug on it. Someone must pull out all of its slack until it gets very tight. Then in human hands, the rubber band can do anything.

"People are like that. We're not really any good all alone. God has to take us, pull us, tug us, and put us under pressure until we are ready and useful. By ourselves we can do nothing.

"The apostle Paul once made a wonderful boast. He said, 'I can do all things through Christ which strengtheneth me.' He didn't claim to do anything alone. Paul recognized that each of us must place ourselves in the hand of God who will strengthen us for His task."

23.

Keep Life's Fire Burning

Interest Object:	A large jar with a lid and a burning candle inside the jar
Main Truth:	Without Jesus life is not long, but with Jesus life is forever.
Scripture Text:	"He who has the Son has life; he who has not the Son of God has not life" (I John 5:12, RSV).

"We must be very careful with fire, but this burning candle is very safe right now within this jar. Just to be safe, I will place the lid on top of the jar. Notice that the candle is still burning because God has provided air in the jar. But it won't burn forever, will it? Soon this flame will use all of the oxygen within the jar. Then it will flicker, fade, and finally die. Let's watch.

"This candle flame reminds me that God has provided everything in life for me to live. Yet I cannot live forever on earth. I am like a candle flame inside the sealed jar. Some day I shall die. Some day you shall die.

"Dying is not so bad if we can live again in a better life. God promises us that if we allow Jesus to come into our lives, then we can live forever. To open the door of your heart and life to Jesus is very much like taking the lid off this jar. Jesus who is God comes from the outside into the inside of our lives. Jesus makes the difference! 'He who has the Son has life; he who has not the Son of God has not life.' "

24.

Size Doesn't Count

Interest Object: A pair of very large men's shoes

Main Truth: With God size does not count, because you are already big enough for His use.

Scripture Text: "So David prevailed over the Philistine with a sling and with a stone, and struck the Philistine, and killed him; There was no sword in the hand of David" (I Sam. 17:50, RSV).

"Here we have a very big pair of shoes. Can anyone of you children possibly wear these shoes? Of course not. They are far bigger than most of you children's feet will ever grow. But so what? Size doesn't count for everything!

"When I was a child your size, I used to daydream about growing up to be a great big man. Then I could do anything. Yet even today I could not fill these big shoes. Does that mean I can't do anything? Definitely not! Size doesn't count when it comes to doing something for God.

"Do you remember the story of the boy David who once killed the giant named Goliath? All of the big soldiers were very afraid of this giant. Yet David as a little shepherd boy knew that size doesn't count for everything. The giant had a big heavy sword, but all little David had were five smooth stones. With God, a small boy and a few stones were enough to kill the giant.

"Even though you may be small right now, God can use you in big ways. You don't have to wait to be big to say kind words, to do good deeds, and to love others. You are big enough right now!"

25.

What Do You Think?

Interest Object: A picture or a bust of Abraham Lincoln

Main Truth: Just as the opinion of the boy Jesus was valued, the opinion of each child is important.

Scripture Text: "And all who heard him were amazed at his understanding and his answers" (Luke 2:47, RSV).

"Here is a picture of one of our favorite presidents with his famous beard. We could hardly think of Mr. Lincoln without his beard, but actually he wore a beard only during the last four years of his life. Do you know when he decided to wear a beard?

"The president was on a train returning to Washington when it stopped at a little town in New York state. Many people were gathered at the train depot to see the president, so Mr. Lincoln stood at the back of the train to give a brief speech. In that crowd an eleven-year-old girl named Grace Bedell. Because Grace was so small, her father held her high so she could see the famous man.

"Guess what! Mr. Lincoln saw her on top of her daddy's shoulder and invited her to climb up on the train with him. When she gave him a hug she felt those stickers which every man has on his chin late in the day. So she said, 'Mr. Lincoln, why don't you grow a beard? You would look nice with one.'

"A few days later Grace Bedell received a letter from President Lincoln. He agreed with her that a beard would be a good idea. So because of the opinion of one little girl, President Lincoln grew his famous beard! I'm very glad that her opinion was important enough for a president to consider.

"When Jesus was just a boy of about twelve years, His parents took Him to Jerusalem. You remember the story of how He somehow became separated from the group. Instead of going back home He went to the temple. All of the wise leaders in the temple were amazed at His understanding and His opinions.

"I'm glad that Jesus didn't wait until He was an adult before He went to the temple. Because He went as a child and they asked His opinion, we adults are reminded that all children and their opinions are important."

26.

The Root of All Evils

Interest Object:	A jar or vase with a coin inside
Main Truth:	We can be trapped by our own greed.
Scripture Text:	"For the love of money is the root of all evils" (I Tim. 6:10a, RSV).

"I once heard of a little boy who was visiting his grandmother when he noticed a vase similar to this. He was very surprised when he peeked inside and noticed a shiny coin in the bottom. About that time, his grandmother reminded him that he wasn't to play in the living room where she had so many expensive vases. So he went outside to play.

"Even though he was outside, do you know what he was thinking about? He couldn't forget seeing that coin in the vase. The more he thought about it, the more he wanted it. He had fallen in love with that coin. Even though he knew it was against his grandmother's command, he slipped back into the house to get the coin for himself.

"When he reached inside the vase he felt the coin with his fingers. It felt so good that he held it tightly. At last he had the coin!

"But what happened when he tried to pull his hand out of the vase? You guessed it. He found his hand was caught inside. Try as he could, the hand would not come out of the jar. Then he became very frightened and called his grandmother who was also very frightened.

"They tried everything, but his hand would not come out. Finally they called the fire department. The fire chief was a wise man and he immediately saw the problem. He asked the little boy what he kept holding in his hand. Finally the boy confessed that he was holding the coin tightly in a fist. The chief said, 'When you let go of that coin, you will be able to pull your hand out of the jar.' And that is what happened. The boy opened his fist, making his hand smaller, and he was set free. He thought he had the coin, but the coin really had him.

"God's Word teaches us that the love of money is the root of all evils. Money itself is not evil, but our love of money is. Some people love money so much that they will do anything for it. They even steal or kill for money. When that happens, money traps them!"

27

No String Attached

Interest Object:	A beautiful candlestick with heavy string attached
Main Truth:	God's gift of salvation through Jesus Christ is free with no strings attached.
Scripture Text:	"For by grace you have been saved through faith; and this is not of your own doing, it is the gift of God" (Eph. 2:8, RSV).

"Would you children like to see and hold this beautiful candlestick? Don't worry about the string attached. Just pretend that it is not even there. Perhaps one of you would even like to hold the candlestick. [After a child holds it for just a moment, the pastor suddenly pulls the string hard enough that the candlestick returns to him.]

"Oops! The candlestick decided to come back into my possession. Let's try it again. [The pastor again gives the candlestick to a child to hold. The second child will begin to catch on by now, so it might be wise to avoid an older child who will be holding very firm in anticipation.]

"It's hard to ignore the string attached to this lovely item, because it prevents you from keeping the item long. Perhaps you've heard the expression 'no strings attached.' That simply means an agreement is made without any secret surprises, unlike this string which took the candlestick away from you.

"I'm glad that God doesn't take back salvation that He gives us just because we do wrong. The apostle Paul reminds us that salvation is free. When Jesus comes into our heart, He remains for as long as He is welcome. He doesn't leave us if we do something wrong. Instead, He remains within us to correct us so we won't do that wrong thing again. Salvation is free. No strings attached!"

28.

Calling God Now

Interest Object:	A telephone
Main Truth:	Like calling a friend, it is easier to pray to God when we are near Him.
Scripture Text:	"Seek the Lord while he may be found, call upon him while he is near" (Isa. 55:6, RSV).

"The telephone is very familiar to us all. Even some of you who do not yet attend school know how to dial the telephone number of your favorite friends. It's easy to call a friend who lives in your neighborhood.

"What happens if you move away from your friend? You probably won't talk very often with him, and thus you may forget his telephone number. Besides that, it is not as easy to telephone long distance as in your own neighborhood, because you must remember more numbers.

"Prayer is very similar to a telephone. Long ago, before the telephone was invented, Isaiah was a prophet for God. He taught people to look for God and pray to Him instantly, rather than waiting. If we wait to talk to God, we may not be as close to Him as we would like to be. People sometimes even forget how to pray.

"You have been taught how to pray. Prayer is simply calling God. May I encourage you to pray often. Before every meal and every bedtime, you ought to pray to God. After all, you know that God is like a good friend who is always listening.

"Don't wait until you have grown up and then try to pray. God will still be listening for you, but it will be harder for you to feel that He is close. Keep in touch with God now!"

29.

To Help A Hurt

Interest Object:	A large bottle of pills plus a "gospill" poster
Main Truth:	For the hurt of sin, the gospel prescribes confession to God.
Scripture Text:	"If we confess our sins, he is faithful and just, and will forgive our sins and cleanse us from all unrighteousness" (I John 1:9, RSV).
Memory Maker:	Large capsules with text printed inside

Notes and Preparation

Your neighborhood pharmacist who knows you well might loan you a large bottle of sample pills used for display purposes. If not, perhaps he has an advertising poster of a large bottle of pills. Ask him also for some large size capsules in which you can put a small Scripture text. As for the "gospill," take a poster board and draw a capsule at least one foot in size. On one side print in bold letters "GOSPILL" and on the other side print "CONFESSION, I John 1:9."

"Here is a very large bottle of pills. It seems that today we have pills available for every possible hurt or pain. If we have a headache, we take an aspirin. If our stomach hurts, we have pills for our tummy.

"We probably take far too many pills for our health. There is one type of hurt which no ordinary pill can possibly help, because it is not an ordinary pain. Whenever we sin, we have a different type of hurt which can be helped only by the 'gospill.'

"Here is that special kind of pill for the hurt of sin. [Hold high the poster display of a gospill.] This is a gospill. On the opposite side is printed God's formula to help the hurt and aches in our heart caused by sin. It says, 'CONFESSION, I John 1:9.''

"The pill is 'confession.' God wants us to confess our sins to Him so He can forgive us of our sins and cleanse us so that we can be healed. This is the formula found in our Scripture text.''

30.

A Pearl for Your Troubles

Interest Object: An oyster and a pearl

Main Truth: In the midst of our troubles God is often making pearls for us.

Scripture Text: "These troubles and sufferings of ours are, after all, quite small and won't last very long. Yet this short time of distress will result in God's richest blessing upon us forever and ever!" (II Cor. 4:17, LB).

Notes and Preparation

An oyster shell is rather common to those living close to the coast or those in larger population centers. Those living inland can use a common, fresh water clamshell just as effectively. The pearl can be artificial or cultured and can even be attached to a tie tack or string of beads.

"Do any of you children ever have troubles such as getting sick or having things bother you? Of course! We all have troubles in life. Let me tell you the story about an oyster who once lived in a shell like this deep in the ocean. Like the turtle, the oyster has a shell which is his home. One day a small grain of sand got inside the shell. Ouch! That hurt the oyster. Because he couldn't rid himself of that grain of sand, the oyster did the next best thing. He decided to live with his trouble.

"Gradually over the months and even years, that grain of sand was coated over and over with a special substance from the oyster. This kept it from hurting so much. The grain of sand grew bigger and bigger until it finally became a pearl. What had begun as trouble, later became a very expensive and beautiful pearl. The oyster was very proud of that pearl!

"Sometimes God uses our troubles to make pearls. For instance, I once knew of a boy who was sick a long time. He was forced to stay in bed during all of the pretty days of summer. For others that would be bad trouble, but this boy used his time in bed to make beautiful airplane models. He became so good at making airplanes that he won a prize worth lots of money. In that way, he turned his troubles into pearls.

"God teaches us that all of our troubles and sufferings are very small and won't last very long. The short time that we are distressed will result in God's best blessings upon us forever. [Close with Scripture text.]"

31.

Many Members but One Body

Interest Object:	Pictures of eye, ear, nose feet, etc.
Main Truth:	All people including children are important as equals, together forming the church.
Scripture Text:	"For just as the body is one and has many members, and all the members . . . are one body, so it is with Christ. Now you are the body of Christ and individually members of it" (I Cor. 12:12, 27, RSV).

Notes and Preparation

For this sermon you will need drawings of an ear, eye, nose, and other members of the body. If you cannot find such pictures, hand drawn displays will be just as good, if not better. Ask someone in your church to draw these on posters large enough to be visible to everyone. Then choose enough children so that each may display one picture before the congregation.

"Today we will ask some volunteers to each hold a picture of a different part of the body. One of you will represent the foot, another will be the nose, another will be the hand, and so on. We are using pictures because no one would want to volunteer giving us their ear or their hand or even their foot! After all, every part of us is very important.

"The apostle Paul once used this same illustration in teaching us that every person in church is very important. [At this point, the pastor might simply open God's Word to I Corinthians 12 and read the excellent illustration which Paul offers.] "

Signs from God
for the Paths of Men

Interest Object:	Posters or copies of traffic signs
Main Truth:	In the Bible are many traffic signs from God for the pathways of life.
Scripture Text:	"Thy word is a lamp to my feet and a light to my path" (Ps. 119:105, RSV).

Notes and Preparation

Traffic signs are a familiar promotional theme. Some commercial institutions give away windshield scrapers in the design of a stop sign ("Stop and do business with me") or key chains shaped like a yield sign ("We yield for our customers"). Specialties like this may make excellent memory makers to give each child.

"Today let's talk about traffic signs. Everyone who wants to drive on our American roads must first learn the meaning of these traffic signs. They are for our safety. Traffic signs will tell us when to stop, when to let the other drivers go first, or when we must slow down.

"Some day you children will take a driver's test to qualify for your driver's license. That means you will be allowed to drive a car. The police officer who helps with this test will ask you the meaning of some of these signs. You will be expected to recognize these signs even without any writing on them. For instance, what kind of sign is this? [The pastor can display a yield symbol or stop symbol without the words on it.]

"I am very glad that we have road signs to help keep us safe. But I am even more glad that God has given His own instructions on how to live. Here is a Bible. It is God's Word with many good rules and warnings which help keep us safe. Listen to how the psalmist described it. 'Thy Word is a lamp to my feet and a light to my path.'

"God does not want us to be ignorant of His safety rules. He does not leave our pathway dark nor our roads of life without good directions. He warns us of dangers ahead and when to stop or go. The Bible contains all these signs from God for the paths of men."

33.

Please Be Patient

Interest Object:	A button or sign worn on the lapel
Main Truth:	We aren't perfect yet because God still isn't finished with us; therefore please be patient.
Scripture Text:	"My dear friends, we are now God's children, but it is not yet clear what we shall become. But this we know: when Christ appears, we shall become like him, because we shall see him as he really is" (I John 3:2, TEV).

Notes and Preparation

A popular little saying these days is "Please be patient; God is not finished with me yet." It can often be found in the form of badges or buttons sold in Christian bookstores. It sometimes comes in the simple initials PBP-GINFWMY designed to make people ask the meaning, so that your testimony can be shared. Any of these buttons will do, or you can simply make your own.

"Is anyone here today perfect? Of course not. When you look into the mirror, are you as pretty as you would like to be? Or as strong? Or as tall? Of course not!

"But wait! God is not finished with you yet. Be patient. That's the simple meaning of this small badge I'm wearing. It helps others realize that I'm not perfect because God is not finished with me.

"This we know. Right now we are God's children, and some day God will make us perfect. Not now, but some day. This is the promise of I John 3:2. [Close by reading this text.]"

34.

God's Special Care for Us

Interest Object:	A pet turtle, bird, rabbit, etc.
Main Truth:	God supplies the needs of all His creatures, especially of Christians.
Scripture Text:	"And my God will supply every need of yours according to his riches in glory in Christ Jesus" (Phil. 4:19, RSV).

"Wouldn't it be a strange world without animals? Throughout God's world are animals such as birds, turtles, rabbits, and even skunks. Did you know that every animal God ever made has been supplied with special care? God has provided food for every animal plus special protection from enemies.

"Here is a turtle. How does the turtle keep safe from his enemies? He simply draws into his shell which is like a fort. Inside of his shell the turtle is safe. Can you guess how the little birds keep safe from their enemies? They have wings to fly. Even the helpless little rabbit has something to keep him safe. He has very fast feet so he can run from his enemies. Of course, the skunk has the best protection of all!

"We are glad that God cares for all His creatures, but we can be even more thankful that God will supply all of our needs. The apostle Paul once told his friends in the church at Philippi: 'And my God will supply every need of yours according to his riches in glory in Christ Jesus.'

"This means that whatever you really need, God will provide. Perhaps He won't provide you with a beautiful bicycle, but that is because we often don't really need things like that. But those special things we need to live and grow stronger for Jesus will always be available. God knows our needs."

35.

Not Void but Good

Interest Object:	Play money, foreign money, and a real United States dollar to compare with a Bible
Main Truth:	God's Word is not void, but is always good.
Scripture Text:	"So shall my word be that goeth forth out of my mouth: it shall not return unto me void, but it shall accomplish that which I please, and it shall prosper in the thing whereto I sent it" (Isa. 55:11).

Children enjoy play money, but they are sharp enough to know the difference between play money and the real thing. Display to them first some play money and ask if they could buy any real candy with it. You will be greeted with a chorus of little voices each saying a loud and firm, no.

Next, show them a foreign bill and tell them it is real money. Then ask them if they could buy candy with it. Again they correctly realize that this money is useless to them. It is *void*. Explain the meaning of that term—"useless, empty, and of no value."

Then produce a real United States bill for their evaluation, and they will all agree that this money is good. It will indeed buy candy. So strong and well accepted is the United States dollar that it will buy candy in any country in the world.

"Why is it good money? Simply because our government says so. The word of our government is good. Everyone knows it. Therefore the United States bill is never void in any place in the world.

"Now let's talk about something that is even more valuable and always good. It is never void. Here is a copy of the Bible. It is God's Word. It is always true, useful, and good. Why? Simply because God says so. Therefore we believe it.

"In Isaiah 55:11, God explains that His Word is never void. Everytime someone reads it, something happens. It never returns void or empty, but always accomplishes what God pleases."

36.

The Crab That Grabs

Interest Object:	A life size rubber crab with ten feet of string
Main Truth:	The most important need in life is God.
Scripture Text:	"But seek ye first the kingdom of God, and his righteousness; and all these things shall be added unto you" (Matt. 6:33).

As the children assemble, the pastor displays the rubber crab and briefly discusses the selfish nature of this little ocean resident. "He eats anything. The crab is so greedy that he should be named 'grab.' He grabs anything that looks like food and is too stubborn to turn it loose.

"If we want to catch the crab, we don't need a hook. We can simply stand on the dock and toss into the water a chicken bone tied by this piece of string. [Pastor demonstrates by placing the crab "in the ocean." A pencil can serve as the "bait" on a string thrown toward the crab. A well practiced twist of the string around the crab's paw will satisfy a child's imagination that the crab has grabbed the bait.] Now watch what happens.

"Slowly we pull the string, but the crab holds on to his prize. He is so selfish that he blindly holds on until it is too late! [Having pulled the string slowly to the "dock," pastor dramatically reaches to grab the crab.] The crab is thus caught not with a hook but through his own blind and selfish greed.

"Some people are like that. They are always grabbing for things in life. They want this. They want that. It's so easy to say, 'Oh, if I can't have it I'll just die!' That is exactly what happens to the crab!

"Of course, that is not really true for us. We can live without most things in life. On the other hand, getting what we want sometimes gets us into a lot of trouble!

"There is nothing wrong with food, clothes, or money, but these things are not the most important things in life. Jesus told us not to worry about what we eat or drink or the clothes we wear. He said the most important thing in the world is God. When we search for God first, these other things are provided. 'Seek ye first the kingdom of God and his righteousness; and all these things shall be added unto you.'"

37.

The Devil's Trap

Interest Object: A rubber mouse and a mouse trap baited with cheese

Main Truth: The devil wants to trap us, but God can keep us safe.

Scripture Text: "Be careful—watch out for attacks from Satan, your great enemy. He prowls around like a hungry, roaring lion, looking for some victim to tear apart. Stand firm when he attacks. Trust the Lord . . ." (I Peter 5:8-9, LB).

Notes and Preparation

A lightweight sheet of plywood or cardboard about 14″ by 18″ makes a convenient background for this sermon. Glue or bolt the trap securely in place on the hand-held board. Not only will this allow adults in the back rows to see the small trap and mouse, but it will also keep little fingers a safe distance away. For further safety and visual effect, tape the little mouse to the tip of a pencil or dowel. A thin knife slit on the pencil or stick will weaken it sufficiently that when the trap springs the tip dramatically snaps off.

Most grownups may prefer a hero other than the mouse, but remember Mighty Mouse? Children are conditioned through comics and cartoons to a hero's role for this small creature.

The main point, however, is the struggle of every believer with the devil who "prowls around like a hungry, roaring lion, looking for some victim to tear apart" (I Peter 5:8). We are to "stand against the wiles of the devil" (Eph. 6:11, RSV).

"Who can tell me what kind of trap we have here? Yes, this is a mouse trap. It is loaded with cheese which mice like to nibble and the trap is ready to spring. Here is a little mouse which I have placed on the end of the stick so you can see him better. This little mouse sees the cheese and would like to eat it. But it doesn't belong to him, so that would be stealing. Is it right to steal? Of course not!

"The little mouse knows it's wrong to steal, but he still wants that cheese. He wonders, 'What harm would come if I nibbled just a little bit? It wouldn't hurt anyone.' Oh, but yes it would. It would hurt the mouse, wouldn't it? Let's see what happens if someone tries to steal the cheese. I'll take the mouse off the end of the pencil and just touch the pencil to the cheese. [With a loud smash the trap springs shut!]

"It would have been very bad for the mouse to try stealing just a little piece of cheese. It's the devil who gives us bad ideas like that. Perhaps you have been in a candy store and thought about taking some candy without paying for it. That would be wrong. You may think that nothing would happen to you, but remember the devil has a trap set for you, too. It's not the same kind of trap, but it's still very dangerous.

"In the Bible we are warned to be careful. Temptations like this come from Satan. [Read the Scripture text at this point.] We are to trust the Lord and stand firm instead of yielding to temptation.

"Remember, the devil would trick us into believing that nothing bad would happen to us if we steal. But even if we don't get caught the first time, we will still be hurt. Wrong will always be punished sooner or later. It is better to trust the Lord, not Satan."

38.

The Door to Your Heart

Interest Object:	A doctor's stethoscope
Main Truth:	God knocks on the door of every heart seeking to enter every life.
Scripture Text:	"Behold, I stand at the door, and knock: if any man hear my voice, and open the door, I will come in to him . . ." (Rev. 3:20).

"Let's talk about something everyone of you has inside your body. It goes duh-dum, duh-dum, every hour and every day of your life. As long as you live, it never stops. What is it?

"We are talking about your heart. You can listen to someone's heart simply by leaning your ear close to the chest. But a doctor uses a stethoscope like this. [Pastor pulls the interest object from his pocket and inserts it in his ears.] This little piece of metal is held on the chest or even the back and the sound travels through these tubes to his ears.

"Do you know what a doctor is listening for? What do these sounds of the heart mean to him? The physicians tell us that a heart is just like a little pump house with doors. The heart pumps the blood throughout the body. The duh-dum sound we hear is caused by the doors opening and closing. Doctors call these little doors 'heart valves.' The back door lets some blood out while the front then opens to let more blood in.

"The doctor listens to these sounds to be sure your heart is opening and closing just right. He can tell by the sound if something is wrong. But let's talk about another kind of door to your heart. The sound associated with this door is a knock when someone wants to come in.

"It is Jesus who knocks on the heart door of every person because He wants to enter into every life. In the Bible we read our text. [From this point the pastor can apply the truth.]"

39.

Thinking Good Thoughts

Interest Objective:	A barrel of apples
Main Truth:	Keep bad thoughts from your mind because they spoil good thoughts.
Scripture Text:	"Finally, brethren, whatever is true, whatever is honorable, whatever is just, whatever is pure, whatever is lovely, whatever is gracious, if there is any excellence, if there is anything worthy of praise, think about these things" (Phil. 4:8, RSV).
Memory Maker:	An apple to take home

Notes and Preparation

You need a barrel of apples for this sermon. Look for a small wooden barrel commonly used to pack nails in a hardware store. Fill it with enough apples to give one per child. If this number will not completely fill the barrel, place an empty box in the bottom first to bring the level very full. Somewhere in the middle of the barrel, place a very bruised and discolored apple. That will serve as the rotten apple. Cover the barrel of apples with a cloth.

After the children are comfortable begin by reading the Scripture text. Emphasize the word *think*. Ask the children why God would want us to think about such good things.

Explain that God wants us to think about these good things and not about bad things. "Good thoughts help us do good deeds, but bad thoughts are just like rotten apples. One rotten apple can spoil a whole barrel of good apples. [Now the pastor pulls the covering from the barrel.]

"Here is a fine barrel of apples which are good to eat. They should last for months except for one fact. Inside this barrel of good apples is one bad apple. Do you know what happens when you leave one bad apple in a barrel of good apples? They all become bad apples. Let's get rid of the bad apple."

The pastor begins looking for the bad apple. As each good apple is brought from the barrel it is passed on to the children to keep as individual memory makers. No need to try creating a dramatic impact when the children find the rotten apple. Children are so naturally expressive and uninhibited that the entire church will enjoy their reaction upon finding the bad apple.

Summarize the main truth again and send the children back to their pews each with an apple and a reminder for them to wait until later to enjoy the apple.

40.

Weighed and Found Wanting

Interest Object: Balance scales

Main Truth: With Jesus we are saved from the balance scales of God.

Scripture Text: ". . . Thou art weighed in the balances, and art found wanting" (Dan. 5:27).

Notes and Preparation

While a genuine balance may be somewhat rare, many homes have ornamental balance scales. They are usually found filled with artificial grape clusters and resting upon the coffee table. For the first demonstration, select a rock or piece of wood wrapped in aluminum foil to serve as the standard weight. A sack of dried beans can be measured produce.

The second demonstration requires a small Bible as the standard and a small doll or toy man to weigh. Use a metal or wood cross as large as possible for visual effect, but be certain the cross and the man balance evenly against the Bible.

"We have here today a set of scales. Unlike our modern scales which measure in pounds and ounces, the oldtime scales could only measure in terms of a balance. Let me demonstrate for you.

"Perhaps you would go to the market to buy one pound of beans for your meal. After agreeing on the price, you must agree on how much is an exact pound. The merchant would take his standard weight which was usually approved by the king or the government and place the one-pound weight on one side of the scale. Then he would pour the produce into the opposite side of the balanced scales. When the sides balance we can be sure that they weigh exactly the same. This process has always been known as 'weighing in the balance.'

"Once the prophet Daniel told the great King Nebuchadnezzar that the king had been weighed in God's balances and was found wanting. That's a frightening thought, but it's true of all of us. Alone we are not good enough to escape God's punishment for our sins. By myself I am doomed because God is a perfect God who must punish sin.

"Let's use this Bible to represent God's judgment toward us. [Place the Bible on one side and the toy man on the other.] See how the man alone is not equal to God's standard of judgment. All the good deeds he can do forever will not make him good enough to balance in God's scales of judgment. He is forever doomed if he is alone.

"I'm glad that we are not weighed alone. We have Jesus on our side. He died for us and now lives for us. If we allow Jesus to come into our hearts we do not have to worry about being found wanting in the balances. This cross can represent Jesus. Watch as we place the cross into the scale with the man. With Jesus the man is found weighed and acceptable."

41.

Working with God

Interest Object: One pair of chopsticks
Main Truth: We work together with God.
Scripture Text: "For we are partners working together for God . . ." (I Cor. 3:9, TEV).
Memory Maker: Souvenir chopsticks for each child

Notes and Preparation

For this sermon the pastor must be acquainted with chopsticks or have written instructions for their use. They can be purchased in quantity from many variety and specialty stores. Note from the instructions that the lower stick remains in place with one part resting upon the ring finger and the other end between thumb and first finger. The higher stick is controlled by action of the thumb and first finger as it drops down against the tip of the bottom stick.

"Do you know what a partner is? This is someone who is always with you. If you are playing, your partner is playing with you. If you are working, your partner is working with you.

"Let's talk about the best partnership of all. This is a partnership with God. Here is our text: 'For we are partners working together for God.' That's an exciting thought! Let's illustrate it with these chopsticks.

"Watch how these chopsticks work together in my hand. Notice that the bottom stick doesn't move at all. The top stick does all the work. That's the way it is when we work together as partners with God. We must be willing to let Him use us. He is the leader and we are His partner. This doesn't mean we never lift a finger to help God. We must indeed be busy doing good deeds as He leads us."

42.

Together for Strength

Interest Object: A handful of dowels from twelve to eighteen inches long and a length of string to tie them together in a bundle.

Main Truth: When we come together at church with Jesus, we become strong.

Scripture Text: ". . . you are members of God's very own family, citizens of God's country, and you belong in God's household with every other Christian. We who believe are carefully joined together with Christ . . ." (Eph. 2:19, 21, LB).

Memory Maker: A dowel for each child

Holding his stick high for everyone to see, the pastor appears in a boastful mood. He claims that his stick is the strongest stick in the whole wide world. No one can break his stick! Does any child want to try?

An invitation like this can't be resisted by any child. Sure enough! On the first try any child you pick will easily break the stick. At this the pastor appears heartbroken. He wonders out loud, "How can I make my stick strong?"

Then the obvious solution comes to him in a flash of inspiration. If one stick alone is weak, perhaps all sticks together will be strong. With a few inches of string, he ties the sticks together and then chooses the biggest boy present.

Can he break the entire bundle of sticks? No individual can overcome this combined strength.

The point is now obvious. "Each of us alone is very weak. But when we meet together in church, we become strong. This is the very reason Jesus wanted us to always attend church. United we stand, divided we fall. We must stay together!

"The apostle Paul once reminded the Christians in Ephesus that they belonged together. He told them, 'You are members of God's very own family, citizens of God's country, and you belong in God's household with every other Christian. We who believe are carefully joined together with Christ. . . .'

"*Together.* That's a wonderful word. When we come together with each other and with Jesus in church, we are no longer weak like this one stick alone. That's why Jesus wants us to always come to church."

43.

You Can't Fool God

Interest Object:	A beautiful wax apple
Main Truth:	We can be tricked and we can trick others, but we can't fool God.
Scripture Text:	"... for the Lord sees not as man sees; man looks on the outward appearance, but the Lord looks on the heart" (I Sam. 16:7, RSV).

Notes and Preparation

Here is another of those childhood memories common to most any pastor. The story can be adapted to your needs or even changed to take another direction.

Wax candles provide a variation of the same truth. I once used a candle molded in an old-fashioned, ice cream soda glass. It looked delicious enough to eat. It fooled the children, especially when I had it freezing cold in the church freezer prior to the sermon.

"This morning I have a beautiful red apple. It reminds me that when I was a little boy, I once went next door to visit my favorite neighbor. She would usually give me cookies, ice cream, or some fruit like this apple to eat. One day I was visiting in her kitchen while she was making cookies. I kept watching this beautiful bowl of fruit on her table. Inside was the most delicious looking apple I had ever seen. Can you guess what I did as soon as she had her back turned?

"You guessed it! I took that apple and tried to take the biggest bite I could. You know what happened? It wasn't a real apple! It was only a wax apple. I was so fooled that I quickly placed the apple back in the bowl. Later she saw my teeth prints and knew I had been fooled.

"It's easy for me to be fooled, and sometimes I might even trick you. One thing, however, we can never do. We just cannot fool God. That's because God doesn't look on the outward appearance like we look at this apple. God looks deeply within and knows what is inside of everything, including our hearts.

"Once God told his prophet Samuel to choose a new king. Samuel saw a young man who was very handsome on the outside. Yet God told Samuel that the handsome man was not right inside. The prophet was told that God looks inside a person. [Read Scripture text.]"

44.

Your Picture of Jesus

Interest Object: A framed picture of Jesus

Main Truth: You are the only picture of Jesus some people will ever see.

Scripture Text: "So God created man in his own image, in the image of God he created him; male and female he created them" (Gen. 1:27, RSV). "And the disciples were called Christians first in Antioch" (Acts 11:26c).

" 'Remember the Alamo' was more than just a slogan to thousands of settlers in Texas who were fighting for their freedom. They could not forget those brave defenders who died in the battle of the Alamo. Some years after that battle, a historical committee began restoring the ruined fort. In the chapel they assembled personal artifacts, letters, and pictures of individual heroes. Today people from all over the world come to that hallowed shrine of Texas liberty to remember those men who died for freedom.

"Colonel James Butler Bonham is among those heroes remembered. He had come from South Carolina to fight along side his best friend, Commander Travis. In the last days before the final attack, Colonel Bonham was sent out at night to escape and bring back help. When no help was available he realized that the fort and its defenders were doomed. Where others would have chosen to remain alive, Colonel Bonham fought his way back into the fort that he might die with his friends for the sake of liberty.

"For the Alamo display which honors his memory, historians sought a picture of the hero. Unfortunately Colonel Bonham had never taken time for a picture or a portrait, but family members solved the problem. They provided a picture of Bonham's own nephew who had been named after him. They all agreed that Major James Bonham II bore a true resemblance to his hero uncle. The inscription on that picture bears a simple testimony.

It is placed here by his family that people may know the appearance of the man who died for freedom.

"How similar is this to the story of Jesus? He is the Son of God who died for our freedom. Whenever we invite Jesus into our hearts we become adopted children of God. Therefore Jesus is our elder brother by adoption. His picture belongs in our family album, but we have no real picture of Jesus. This picture which we see here represents how an artist thought Jesus may have looked.

"Remember that the Bible teaches us that we are created in God's own image. In Acts 11:26 we learn of an important name given to people who believe in God. 'And the disciples were called Christians first in Antioch.' They were named after Jesus Christ. Don't you think this was because they looked and acted like Christ? People in Antioch did not know what Christ looked like, but they could see Christ in the faces of those early Christians. Therefore they called those first followers of Christ, Christians.

"This means that you can become a picture of Jesus for other people. [Pastor takes the picture of Jesus out of the frame and then lifts the open frame to his face.] If you have accepted Jesus as your Savior, your name is Christian. You may be the only picture of Jesus that some people will ever see."

45.

Void if Detached

Interest Object:	A perforated ticket for an airplane, movie, football game, etc.
Main Truth:	When separated from Jesus we are useless and alone.
Scripture Text:	"For without me ye can do nothing" (John 15:5c).

Notes and Preparation

If you have not saved the colorful folder from your last airline ticket, you can use any type coupon book. Simply use your own imagination and draw a picture of an airplane with a magic marker. Paste this over the cover of the coupon book. Of course, the sermon can focus upon a movie passbook, season tickets for football, or any other tickets available.

"Whenever you children attend a football game or a movie, someone standing at the entrance will ask for your ticket. It is the same when we travel by bus, railroad, or even by airplane. Whatever the type ticket we may have, the attendant will tear it in half, returning part as our receipt. It is called a ticket stub. Sometimes this torn half will have our seat number written on it.

"We are not supposed to tear the ticket ourselves. Very often on a ticket is written a simple warning: "Void if detached." This means that if we tear the ticket from the ticket book ourselves, it is no longer any good. It becomes void or without value. Only the ticket taker can tear it out at the proper time.

"The reason for this is so that you won't use the ticket more than once. Whenever the ticket taker detaches it, the ticket becomes void because it has been used. Now what would happen if *you* tore out the ticket? He wouldn't know for certain if your ticket was good. He probably would think your ticket had already been used. Then he wouldn't let you in!

"Some things just have to stay together if they are to be worth anything. Jesus once said, 'For without me ye can do nothing.' He meant that we belong to Him and He belongs to us. If we are separated from Jesus then we can do nothing. We are like only half a ticket."

46.

Let's Cooperate!

Interest Objects: Three heavy suitcases and a strong broom handle

Main Truth: Through cooperation we work together to achieve the difficult.

Scripture Text: "Go ye therefore, and teach all nations, baptizing them in the name of the Father, and of the Son, and of the Holy Ghost: Teaching them to observe all things whatsoever I have commanded you: and, lo, I am with you alway, even unto the end of the world. Amen" (Matt. 28:19-20).

As the children move to the front in the morning service, the pastor removes a cloth to expose three large suitcases neatly lined in a row upon the platform. Each suitcase was previously filled and weighted beyond the strength of any one child. A poster printed in large letters contains the two verses of Christ's Great Commission (Matt. 28:19-20) with the words *go, teach,* and *baptize* underlined. Each of these commands represents a duty for every Christian. Like suitcases, these three duties are each to be carried out in life's journeys. The responsibility is very heavy.

At this point the pastor invites any of the children to lift all or even one of the weighted suitcases. It is too big a task.

"Then how can we possibly carry out our duty? Could we work together by cooperating?" he asks.

A long, sturdy stick (broom handle) best symbolizes this idea of working together. It is inserted through the three suitcase handles, making a way for the children to cooperate. Every child somehow finds a hand-hold, and at the count of three the impossible is experienced. Lifting high the heavy burdens with little effort but great enthusiasm, the children again prove that through cooperation we Christians can be strong indeed.

47.

Who Gives the Most?

Interest Object: A large, clear jar filled with candy and a smaller jar with only two pieces.

Main Truth: The amount we give God is measured by how much we keep for ourselves.

Scripture Text: "And Jesus sat over against the treasury, and beheld how the people cast money into the the treasury: and many that were rich cast in much. And there came a certain poor widow, and she threw in two mites, which make a farthing. And he called unto him his disciples, and saith unto them, Verily I say unto you, That this poor widow hath cast more in, than all they which have cast into the treasury: For all they did cast in of their abundance; but she of her want did cast in all that she had, even all her living" (Mark 12:41-44).

Children coming to hear this sermon are welcomed by the pastor with a large candy jar filled with jelly beans. As he offers candy to each of the children, the pastor explains his generous sharing as one way of expressing his love for them. In the same way we give money at church because we love God, and love is always generous.

While the pastor emphasizes his generosity in giving away so much candy, the music minister (or other assistant) timidly interrupts with a request. "Pastor, I have some candy which I would like to share also. May I?" He lifts high his very small jar containing only two jelly beans which he then shares.

Now the question as posed by the pastor is, "Who gave the most?" Naturally the children all point to the pastor, but he pauses to think aloud: "I had much candy before giving any away, and even now I can't really miss any because I still have so much left. Now look at his jar. It's empty. He kept none for himself, but gave it all away. So who really gave the most?

"Jesus taught us that the way to measure how much we give is to see how much we keep for ourselves. We remember this from a story in the Bible which is found in the Gospel of Mark, chapter 12. Jesus was in the temple and saw some rich men giving their money. They must have been very happy because they were giving large amounts of money. But then a very poor woman came along. Although she had only two small coins, she gave them both to God. She kept nothing for herself.

"Now who gave the most—the rich men or the poor woman? Jesus said that the poor woman gave more than all the rich men together because they never missed what they gave away. Like the jar of jelly beans their pockets were still full. But the poor woman, keeping nothing for herself, gave all her money to God. She gave the most.

"This means that your gift is important. God is happy with your gift, even if it does not seem very much. Indeed, if you give to God more than you keep for yourself, then yours is a very big gift. Remember that God knows not only how much we give, but how much we keep."

48.

Don't Forget the Inside

Interest Objects: A worn coffee mug, a nice everyday cup, and a beautiful china cup.

Main Truth: God wants us to be clean inside.

Scripture Text: "Woe to you, Pharisees, and you religious leaders—hypocrites! You are so careful to polish the outside of the cup, but the inside is foul with extortion and greed. Blind Pharisees! First cleanse the inside of the cup, and then the whole cup will be clean. Woe to you, Pharisees, and you religious leaders! You are like beautiful mausoleums—full of dead men's bones, and of foulness and corruption. You try to look like saintly men, but underneath those pious robes of yours are hearts besmirched with every sort of hypocrisy and sin" (Matt. 23:25-28, LB).

As the children come forward they are welcomed by the pastor holding a tray of three coffee cups covered by a cloth. He asks, "Suppose I were to invite all of you to my home? I know what your mother would do. She would look you over carefully to be sure your clothes were neat and your face clean! Mothers are just like that, aren't they? I wonder if God is like that? After all, this church is His home. This morning let's talk about being clean.

"Now when you come to visit me, I may offer you a cup of hot chocolate. Which cup do you prefer?" The pastor lifts the tray of cups slightly above eye level and removes the cloth. Which will they choose—a worn mug, an average cup, or the elegant china cup? Even the children will by a vast majority select on the basis of outside beauty. But watch their expressions change dramatically when he tilts the cup for them to see the unsightly residue. (Traces of chocolate syrup, mustard, and catsup left to dry a few days leave the desired stains.)

Then comes the application: "We were all looking at the outside of the cup, but don't forget the inside. It's the same way with people. Jesus once used this very same illustration to describe some people who considered themselves so good and clean.

> Woe to you, Pharisees, and you religious leaders—hypocrites! You are so careful to polish the outside of the cup, but the inside is foul with extortion and greed. Blind Pharisees! First cleanse the inside of the cup, and then the whole cup will be clean.

"And it's the same with us. God wants us to be clean on the inside as well as the outside. After all, isn't the inside where God likes to live?

"Obviously we cannot take soap and water to clean the heart, but we can ask God to come in and sweep out all the bad thoughts. He will also forgive us whenever we do bad deeds and feel bad inside. But we must first ask Him. Remember, don't forget the inside. Let's pray right now that God will help us be clean inside."